Machu Picchu:
Rediscovering the Mystery of the Incan Land

Table Of Contents

Introduction

Chapter 1 The History Of Machu Picchu

Chapter 2 When to travel

Chapter 3 The Mysteries of Machu Picchu

Chapter 4 What to expect on the Incan trail

Chapter 5 Things to see and do in Machu Picchu

Chapter 6 Traveling to Machu Pichu

Conclusion

Check Out My Other Books

Copyright

Copyright © 2014 Elisabeth Sanz

All rights reserved. No part of this book may be reproduced in any form or by any electronic or mechanical means including information storage and retrieval systems – except in the case of brief quotations in articles or reviews – without the permission in writing from its publisher, Elisabeth Sanz
All brand names and product names used in this book are trademarks, registered trademarks, or trade names of their respective holders. We are not associated with any product or vendor in this book.

Introduction

I want to thank you and congratulate you for downloading the book, Machu Picchu: Rediscovering the Mystery of the Incan Land

This book contains everything you need to know about traveling to Machu Picchu. You will learn the best time to travel, what you will see on different trails, the history of the Incas, what you will find in Machu Picchu and so much more.

If you are considering traveling to Machu Picchu this book is a must have. Containing little known destinations in and around Machu Picchu, you will be sure to have the best vacation and not miss anything that Machu Picchu has to offer.

Thanks again for downloading this book, I hope you enjoy it!

Chapter 1

Machu Picchu means the "old peak" and is found in the Cusco Region, Urubamba Province, Machupicchu District in Peru. Construction of Machu Picchu began in 1450 but the estate was abandoned a century later at the time of the Spanish conquest. The construction of Machu Picchu like many other Inca projects was never completed and was abandoned around 1532 when the Spanish conquistadors arrived in Peru.

Most archeologists think that Machu Picchu was built for the Incan emperor Pachacuti.

Johan Reinhard has presented evidence that the site of Machu Picchu was chosen because of the surrounding sacred landscape features such as the mountains that seem to be in line with astronomical events that were important to the Incas.

Some also believe that in addition to Machu Picchu being the estate of the Emperor Pachacuti that it was also used as a protected source of coca.

Coca was used by the Incas for religious purposes and is used by locals to this day. Many believe that chewing on a coca leave or steeping it in tea will help relieve altitude sickness.

It was customary in the Incan culture that when a ruler died a new estate was built for the new ruler, many speculate that this is why Machu Picchu fell. Still others believe that the water supply may have dried up or the Incas contracted small pox from the Spanish.

Although Bingham was the first to bring attention to the ruins of Machu Picchu, it has been speculated that it was discovered much earlier. The first account reported was in 1901 when three researchers supposedly carved their names in the stones at Machu Picchu. Again in 1904 an engineer is said to have spotted the ruins while on another mountain. He told a Christian missionary who supposedly in 1906 climbed up to the ruins with a fellow missionary.

Historians have found maps which refer to Machu Picchu as early as 1874 so it truly is unclear who discovered it. Bingham had told an amazing story about his discovery of Machu Picchu but later his son uncovered letters that spoke of a much easier discovery. The letters were to Bingham's wife and talked about how he had followed a clear path to Machu Picchu. Bingham had also told the public that Machu Picchu was overrun with brush but his son found photos that showed the opposite. It was also discovered that there were a few families living at Machu Picchu at the time Bingham visited.

Bingham initially stayed at Machu Picchu for only an hour before returning to his camp, he only decided to investigate further because he was told by a local farmer that there was little information about the area.

Machu Picchu is divided into an agricultural sector and an urban sector. The urban sector is divided into two, the upper town and the lower town. In the upper town you will find all of the temples and in the lower town are things such as the warehouses.

There are around 200 buildings in Machu Picchu that are organized on wide corresponding terrenes around a large center square. Machu Picchu has an extensive irrigation system that provided water to the fields as well as several stone stair cases that provide access to the different levels of the city.

It is speculated that the eastern part of the city was the residential area and the western part was used for religious or ceremonial purposes. There is also a large tower in the western part of Machu Picchu that may have been used for a lookout tower or an observatory.

Architecture

The Incans were masters of an architecture style called ashlar which was the cutting of blocks of stones so that they would fit together without the use of mortar. This was done so perfectly that it is said not even a blade of grass could fit between the stones.

Because Machu Picchu was built between two fault lines, the seismic activity deemed mortar useless to the Incans but the Incas developed a way to cut the stones so they fit perfectly together without having to use mortar.

In addition to earthquakes Machu Picchu receives large amounts of rain which led to mud slides and flooding. The Incas found that by using the left over chips of stone they could create a system that would ensure the mountain stay in place.

The Incas built terraces of several different layers. The first layer of the terraces was made of top soil followed by dirt. The dirt was followed by sand which was topped with the stone chips. This ensured that the water would sift down into the mountain instead of running down the mountain creating mud slides.

The Incas build more than 14,000 miles of road, 600 terraces, 16 fountains, several temples and thousands of stairs all out of huge blocks of stone. Some fountains contained over 20 tons of stone. It is also believed that the Incas did this without the use of the wheel.

While the wheel was used in toys found in Machu Picchu there have been no discoveries of the wheel being used to move stones. It is believed that because of the slope of the mountain the wheel would have been ineffective for the Incans. Most archeologists think that the Incans moved the large stones by having several men push them and yet others believe that the remaining knobs left of some of the stones suggest that they stones were lifted into place.

There are also those who believe that Machu Picchu was built with the help of extraterrestrials. No matter how Machu Picchu was built, that fact is that it still remains. It is still a great place of mystery and is one of the most significant historical monuments in the world.

In July 2007 Machu Picchu was declared on of the Seven Wonders of the World joining other sites such as the Great Wall of China.

Currently Machu Picchu is listed on the 100 most endangered sites in the world due to environmental degradation.

The Sacred Valley tour is often included when you visit Machu Picchu. The Sacred Valley is located between Pisac and Ollantaytambo. Composed of many rivers and valleys the Sacred Valley has numerous archeological monuments.

The Sacred Valley was one of the main production sites for the Incas, because the microclimates allow the production of a variety of produce and the rivers are full of trout.

The Sacred Valley begins 15 miles north-east of Cusco and continues northwest for 35 miles.

Who are the Incas?

The Incan language is called Quechua and is still spoken today by many people in the Andes. It is not known what language the Incas spoke before Quechua was officially made their language by Pachacuti in 1438. One amazing fact about the Incans is that instead of writing down their records they used colored knots instead. These colored knots are referred to as quipu.

The Incas worship the sun god and believed that the leader of the Incas who was called the INCA was a divine descendant of this god. The Inca was the absolute power of the Incan world.

The Incan culture began to spread in the 12th century and in only 400 years the Incas controlled a larger part of South America than any other group has controlled.

The culture was spread through concurring other groups and installing local leaders into the government. The Incas gave special treatment to those who did not resist being concurred, and were known to be very generous to those who fought against intruders.

During the time of the Incas there was more cultivated land in the Andean highlands than there is today.

It is thought that the Incas are descendants from the Quechua tribe. Quechua people have dark skin, straight black hair, and rarely had any facial hair.

The Incans diet consisted of a lot of white potatoes and very little meat because the llamas and alpacas were too valuable for the Incas to eat unless the animal died of old age.

The Inca considered Cusco to be the spiritual center of the Incan universe and made it their capital.

The Incas are best known for their feats in engineering, road building, and architectural achievements like those in Machu Picchu.

Truly understanding the Incas is very difficult because they wrote nothing down and all of their stories were passed down orally from one generation to the next. What is known about the Inca people comes from Inca Garcilaso de la Vega who was the son of a Spanish Conquistador and an Inca Princess. He learned Inca traditions and legends from his uncles and later turned them into The Royal Commentaries of the Inca. It is suspected that Christian and European influences may have affected his writing but it is the only look into the Inca world that we have.

It is known that the Inca fell into a civil war that lasted until the Spanish arrived in 1532. When the Spanish arrived they were in search of gold and silver. The Spanish therefore melted a lot of the Incan art and metalwork.

In 1572 Tupac Amaru the last of the Inca was captured by the Spanish, taken to Cusco and beheaded in front of a mass of people by a Cañari Indian.

More recently

In 2008 eighty skeletons and stores of textiles were found in mass graves near Machu Picchu. Mostly the heads and shoulders were uncovered because the Inca buried their dead sitting up in the fetal position.

The remains that were found dated back to between 500 to 550 years before they were found but due to widespread looting 75% of the fabrics that were used to wrap the bodies are in bad shape.

From the wrappings that were made of vegetable fiber, and the simple graves, scientists believe that what they found was the tomb of peasant farmers.

It is very rare to find human remains near Machu Picchu and the wet climate makes finding textiles very uncommon which made this find very significant.

In 2012 a tomb was found that was thought to belong to a high ranking member of the Incan empire. The tomb was uncovered on a hill facing the wall of Machu Picchu. There were no bones or artifacts found inside of the tomb due to the raiding that took place before Machu Picchu was protected.

In June of 2014 a new section of the Incan road to Machu Picchu was discovered. Covered in vegetation, reports state that this road leads directly to Machu Picchu and contains 16.5 feet of tunnel that is still intact over 500 years after it was constructed.

Chapter 2
When to Travel

Deciding when to travel to Machu Picchu is very important and should be thought out before booking a trip.

The Climate

When hiking the Incan trail to Machu Picchu you should be fully aware of the strong seasonal weather. Machu Picchu is known for its wet season but most tourists for obvious reasons prefer to visit during the dry season which is from May to September.

The dry season in Machu Picchu provides tourists with sunny weather and clear skies. The mild weather is accentuated by the elevation of Machu Picchu but due to the elevation nights can become extremely cold with temperatures reaching near freezing at times.

Due to the lack of rain in the dry season, many tourists visit Machu Picchu and the busiest months tend to be July and August.

Machu Picchu Weather By Month

Month	Low	High
January	63 °F	79 °F
February	64 °F	82 °F
March	61 °F	81 °F
April	59 °F	77 °F
May	55 °F	72 °F
June	52 °F	68 °F
July	50 °F	66 °F
August	54 °F	68 °F
September	54 °F	70 °F
October	54 °F	72 °F
November	55 °F	75 °F
December	61 °F	79 °F

Between the months of December and March it is rainy in Machu Picchu but tours are still conducted. Many tourist companies state that as long as you bring a rain coat and an umbrella you will be perfectly fine.

If you decide to travel in the rainy weather it is best to take a train to Machu Picchu instead of hiking the Incan trail. This is because the Incan trail presents its own set of challenges without the addition of rain. When you hike the trail you must hike over 36 miles scale two mountain passes (13,000 feet) which include Dead Woman's Pass.

When you take a train to Machu Picchu you still hike about 4 miles to the gate entrance of Machu Picchu.

Prices

Prices tend to be lower right after the rainy season in Machu Picchu and there tends to be less people taking tours during this period. The weather is nice during this time. (April and May) The Incan Trail to Machu Picchu is closed during the month of February which is the rainiest month of the wet season. Machu Picchu is still accessible by train during this time.

Prices for the Inca trail may vary dramatically ranging from $320 USD for a student to $1200 USD. The lowest prices are usually found during early April or late September because these times are not in the peak season. Booking at these times will also ensure that you miss the rainy season in Machu Picchu.

If you must visit Machu Picchu during the busy season it is very important that you book your trip months in advance because they book very quickly. This also means that you will most likely miss out on some great deals that could save you a ton of money.

If you really want to save some money on your trip you should email several different travel agencies and ask for information and prices. This will benefit you in two ways, one you will get to see how professional they are by how they reply to you or if they reply to you, and two usually by emailing the companies they will offer you a discounted price than what is listed on their website.

If you are visiting in the low season you do not have to worry about booking your Inca trail tour ahead of time. You can actually book it once you arrive in Cusco. You should also allow yourself a few days to get acclimated to the altitude before going on your Incan trail tour.

What you should receive from a travel agency

It is very important to understand what is included for the fees you pay the travel agency. You do not want to be caught on the trail without food or a sleeping bag so it is very important that you ask a few questions.

Ask

- How many people per tour guide? (this should be between 8-10)
- Do the guides speak English?
- Will there be a briefing before you leave? (There should be a briefing the day of departure)
- How much extra cash should you bring?
- If you are renting a sleeping bag from the agency it is very important to know how warm it is.
- Where your campsites are located and how early you should expect to arrive at Machu Picchu

Most agencies should include the following:

- All of your camping gear except for your sleeping back which you should be able to rent for around $3 USD per day.
- All meals for the entire trip except for breakfast on the first day and lunch on the last day.
- Porters who will carry all of the camping and cooking gear. They will not carry your clothing or personal items, this is up to you to carry.

- Fees for the entrance to the Incan trail and Machu Picchu
- A bus ticket to start the trail and one back to Cusco at the end of the tour.

What is not included:

- Sleeping bags. You can rent one from the travel agency or you can bring your own. You want to ensure that you have a thick warm sleeping bag because the nights can get very cold.
- Tips for the porters, guides and cooks.
- Snacks
- A bus ticket for the trip down from Machu Picchu to Aguas Calientes where you board the train for Cusco. This can be walked but takes around one and one half hours.

In the following chapters we will discuss the different things you can do on your tour, places you can stay or visit, and things you will see as well as the mysteries of Machu Picchu.

Chapter 3
The Mysteries of Machu Picchu

The wrong lost city

When Bingham discovered Machu Picchu in 1911 he thought it was Vilcabamba which is the so called lost city of the Inca. For almost 50 years after his discovery Bingham argued that Machu Picchu was the lost city and many accepted his argument.

What Bingham had discovered was in fact not The Lost City but a lost city. In 1964 it was discovered that Espiritu Pampa was the lost city that Bingham had sought after. Bingham had actually discovered the ruins in Espiritu Pampa in 1911 uncovering a few stones but decided it was not large enough to be the lost city and focused on Machu Picchu.

What Bingham had really discovered was a city that had no records of it anywhere. There was no record of Machu Picchu ever existing and no one knew what its purpose was.

Bingham theorized that Machu Picchu was the city for the virgins of the sun where women who devoted their lives to the sun god lived. This was because he found more than 100 skeletons at the site and 75 percent of them were thought to be women. It was later discovered by the use of modern science that there was more of a 50/50 split between men and women.

More recently it has been discovered that Machu Picchu is much smaller than other Inca cities only large enough for around 500 people. It has been thought that Machu Picchu was built as a sort of resort for the elite to get away from the noise and commotion in the larger cities.

Recent excavation has uncovered a secret entrance that leads to the center of the city where many underground rooms have been found. With the use of computers it has been discovered that these rooms are behind a sealed door and contain gold and other precious metals.

Machu Picchu Myths and Legends

There is one legend that explains how the Incas were able to move such large stones without the use of modern technology. The legend says that Viracocha the creator of the Inca caused a huge fire and then extinguished it in order to demonstrate his power to the Inca people. After the stones were burnt they became as light as a cork so that even huge stones could be lifted with ease.

Since the Spanish never found Machu Picchu, a "myth" began to spread that there was gold and treasure hidden under the city and that Machu Picchu was once covered in gold. Many people think this was made up by the Spaniards after finding gold in other cities but recent discoveries show that there is gold under the city so whether this is a myth or not remains to be seen.

Aliens helped the Incas create Machu Picchu. There is still a myth going around today that aliens had something to do with the architecture in Machu Picchu but do not let the locals hear you speak of this because they are very proud of what the Machu Picchu accomplished.

The Inca believed that their creator Viracocha first created a world that was populated by giants that he had fashioned from stone. These giants were disobedient so Viracocha destroyed them and created a new race made out of clay. Before the people populated the world Viracocha told them to sink into the earth than reappear again. The people did this and built a shrine at the spot where they emerged.

Like many people, the Inca also have a story about a great flood. The story states that in the time of the flood people were evil and cruel. The refused to pay the proper attention to the Inca gods. It is said that one day a llama told two shepherds that a flood was coming. The two shepherds gathered their families and livestock and took them to high caves where they waited. It rained for months and the world below them drowned. Finally the sun appeared again and dried the waters. The Inca believe that even though people live everywhere now, the llamas remember the flood and this is why they only live in the high places.

What is the true mystery about Machu Picchu?

The true mystery of Machu Picchu is that no one really knows why it was built or what it was used for. It has been recognized as a secrete place, and many people describe a very spiritual feeling when they go to Machu Picchu. It is only speculation that Machu Picchu was a city built for the elite, or a place that the Inca would retreat to in the event of an invasion.

In reality what Machu Picchu means is something that each person must decide for themselves. It is an experience like no other.

Fun Facts about Machu Picchu

- Machu Picchu has been used as a landing pad for a helicopter twice. Both times the Monolith Stone that was located in the center of Machu Picchu had to be removed in order to allow the helicopters to land, only the second time the stone was broken beyond repair and it was decided that the stone should be buried.

- Two women actually claim that they own Machu Picchu. Roxana and Victoria Abril are two Peruvian sister's that claim that they are the rightful owners of Machu Picchu. They say that their great great grandfather purchased the land before it was rediscovered by Bingham in 1911 and are very upset that they have to pay to be on their own land. They are currently suing the Peruvian government for one hundred million dollars as well as compensation of future profits made by the land mark.

- In early 2014 two men were arrested for streaking across Machu Picchu completely naked afterwards they tried to bribe the guards not to turn them over to the police. Around that same time, two other tourists were arrested for taking naked pictures of each other at Machu Picchu.

- In 2008 during the filming of a beer ad, the upper corner of the Intihuatana Stone was damaged beyond repair when the arm of a crane fell on it. It turned out the group did not have official permission to bring heavy equipment into Machu Picchu.

- Nothing of any archeological importance was ever found at Machu Picchu. Known as one of the most important archeological finds, nothing of any historical importance was ever found at Machu Picchu. This is believed to be because of looting that took place before the area was secured. Another possibility is that the

Incas simply took everything with them, including their mummies.

- Machu Picchu really was not the most important city in the Incan world. Actually Cusco was the capital of the empire, and was a place that had many temples, shrines and magnificent palaces.

- The Incas were able to bring fresh fish from the coast to Machu Picchu in only 24 hours.

- The staff at Machu Picchu is very superstitious. Take for example the porters who travel along the trails with the tours, at night they sleep with mirrors under their tents in order to ward off evil spirits.

- Each year the Incan trail is the host to a race. Once a year runners race along the 26 mile trail. The shortest time it has taken a runner to get to Machu Picchu was three hours and twenty-six minutes.

- You will be detained if you try to enter Machu Picchu while wearing the traditional attire of another country. No kilts allowed here gentlemen!

- You must pay in cash for everything once you reach Cusco. No credit cards are accepted and there are no ATM machines!

Chapter 4
What to Expect on the Inca Trail

The Inca Trail to Machu Picchu actually consist of three overlapping trails. These are Mollepata, Classic, and One Day. The Mollepata trail is the longest of the three. There are many ruins located along the trail including tunnels and settlements all before even reaching the Sun Gate at Machu Picchu.

Due to concerns of erosion due to the amount of people hiking these trials, the Peruvian government has placed a limit to the amount of people who are allowed to hike this trail each season. The government has also limited the companies that can provide tours. The daily limit of people allowed to hike this trail per day is 500 with 300 of those people being guides and porters.

As a result of the limitations the government has put on the trails the high season books up very quickly.

The Classic Trail

It usually takes between four to five days to complete the classic trail. The classic trail will start from one of two points either 55 miles from Cusco or 51 miles from Cusco along the Urubamba River at about 8700 ft. altitude.

Both starting points end at the same place, Llaqtapata which was used for religious and ceremonial purposes, crop production, and housing for soldiers from Willkaraqay. Willkaraqay is a pre-Inca site that was inhabited around 500BC. At the village of Wayllapampa which consists of around 400 people or 130 families, the Classic trail intersects the Mollepata trail at approximately 9800 ft.

At Wayllapampa, the Classic trail will turn west and begin to ascend along a branch of the Kusichaka. Due to previous damage that has been caused by pack animals they are not allowed on the rest of the trail. Neither are metal tipped walking sticks allowed on this part of the trail.

As the trail ascends toward Dead Woman's Pass, it passes through several types of habitats. One habitat the Classic trail will pass through is called the Cloud Forrest. Which is simply a region with constant cloud cover where the clouds actually dip down into the forest itself. This creates a very moist, misty, and dim environment. The campsite Llulluchapampa is located on this stretch of the trail.

After crossing the pass which is located 13,829 ft. above sea level and is the highest point on the trail, the trail begins to drop dramatically into Pakaymayu drainage.

Only one mile below the pass is Pakaymayu campsite. After passing the campsite, the Classic trail begins a steep accent. A little over a half of a mile up the trail at an altitude of 12,300 ft., you will be able to see the Incan tampu Runkuraqay ruins that overlook the valley. The Incan tampu Runkuraqay ruins were heavily restored in the 1990's.

As the trail continues to ascend, you will pass a small lake that is known for as a deer habitat that is called Quchapata. This site used to be used as a campsite but due to overuse, the area is no longer allowed to be used for camping.

The trail continues often steeply though cloud forests, but allows dramatic views of the surrounding mountains and drop-offs. Next you will reach Sayaqmarka followed by Qunchamarka. You will also pass a long Incan tunnel as well as a viewpoint that overlooks the two valleys Urubamba and Aobamba.

After a short distance you will reach Phuyupatamarka which was actually discovered by Bingham. Bingham left most of Phuyupatamarka covered with vegetation which was later cleared out by the Fejos team. The design of the sight follows the curve of the mountain. Phuyupatamarka contains five fountains and an alter which was most likely used for llama sacrifice.

Upon leaving Phuyupatamarka the trail descends about 330 feet, and includes a staircase of 1500 steps. Many of these steps were carved out of solid granite. The vegetation will become much more jungle like and there will be many more birds and butterflies on this part of the trail. There is also a second Incan tunnel along this section of the trail.

After passing through the tunnel, you will be able to see the town of Aguas Calientes and you will be able to hear the trains that run alongside of the river. As you near Intipata you will be able to see views from the One Day trail.

Intipata was recently uncovered and is an extensive set of terraces where potatoes, maize, sweet potatoes and fruit were grown. Next you will see the ruins of Wiñay Wayna which is the name of not only the Inca ruins but the hotel, campsite, and restaurant.

Wiñay Wayna contains a long row of fountains or ritual baths that utilize as many as 19 springs that flow in between the two buildings in Wiñay Wayna. Continuing on from Wiñay Wayna the trail leads eastern side of the mountain called Machu Picchu.

A steep set of stairs leads into the sun gate, and the ruins of Machu Picchu are only a short downhill walk which is the end of the Classic trail.

The Mollepata Trail

The Mollepata trail is a great option for those who want to do a longer trek to Machu Picchu but want an alternative to the Incan trail due to availability of spots.

Depending on the company you go with this trek can last anywhere from four to seven days. We are going to discuss the five day trek.

Since this trek enters the original Inca trail you will have to obtain an Inca trail permit for this trek. And depending on what time of the year you go you may need to book this trail a few months in advance.

Most often the tour guides will take you by buss to Mollepata from Cusco which is about a three and one half hour drive. So on day one you will drive from Cusco to Limatambo where you will visit the ruins of Tarawasi which is a tiered ceremonial platform which features elegant Inca stonework.

Continuing up a side road you will reach Mollepata and just a short distance from Mollepata you will reach Cruz Pata where you will meet your trail team, pack animals and make your first camp.

On day two you will hike over a ridge through the forest and come to the Rio Blanco valley. Following its upper slopes, you will cross the rim of Soraypampa to the open grasslands of the highland puna.

At 13,120 ft., you will cross a broad plateau at the Humantay. As you make camp you will see the ice-covered face of Salcantay which is one of the peaks of the Andes.

Day three is the most challenging day of your hike. You will wind your way past a gigantic terminal moraine that was cause by receding glaciers. Then you will make your accent to the pass of Incachiriasca (16,070ft) Around mid-day you should cross the pass reaching a point called Japanese camp. From there you will descend down into the valley of Sisaypampa. You camp there.

Day four will be a gentle hike downhill to where you will go through Pampacahua and pass the village of Huayllabamba reaching the settlement Patallacta in the afternoon. On day four you will camp at lower altitudes, 8,200ft near the Inca terraces of Q'ente.

On Day five you will catch the train to Aguas Calientes taking a bus to Machu Picchu and should arrive at mid-morning.

As you can tell this is a much more difficult trek than the classic trek and you do not arrive at Machu Picchu in the morning so you will not be able to see the sunrise in the sun gate when you reach Machu Picchu.

The one day trail

If you want to arrive on foot to Machu Picchu and avoid the crowds that arrive by train or bus, the one day trail may be the perfect option for you. You will get off of the train half an hour before arriving at Aguas Calientes then you will hike to the Machu Picchu. Most of the hike is uphill and with a reasonable amount of cliffs. On the way you will visit Wiñay Wayna, an extraordinary Inca site that is only accessible on foot. Upon arrival to Machu Picchu you will be able to explore the ruins before returning to your hotel for the evening. The total hike covers roughly 7.5mi which is around six to seven hours of hiking.

The one day trail is also great for those who were unable to book the Classic trail or those who would rather not spend days hiking.

You always have the option of taking the train and bus to Machu Picchu where you will only have a short walking distance before you enter the sun gate.

Each of these trails range in price from a few hundred dollars per day to a few thousand dollars per day so you want to check your budget before you set your mind on a specific trail.

There are actually six alternative routes to Machu Picchu, these are just three choices. The other routes include:

- The Salcantay Route- 20,500-feet at its highest point and lasts from 5-8 days. Difficulty level is medium to difficult.

- The Lares Route-18,000-plus feet at its highest point and lasts from 3-5 days. Difficulty level is medium.

- Vilcabamba Traverse Route lasts between 7-13 days and the difficulty level is difficult.

- The Lodge Trek- 15,000 feet at its highest point and lasts between 7-11 days. Difficulty level is medium.

- The Chaski (or Cachicata) Trail lasts from 3-5 days and the difficulty level is medium.

Most of these alternative trails require no permits and can easily be arranged through one of the reputable companies in Cusco. There are also hikes available that can be tailored to fit different fitness levels.

Tips for those taking the trails to Machu Picchu

- Avoid packing too much in your backpack.
- Pack a light weight rain poncho.
- Make sure to pack bug spray and sunscreen.
- Bring clear resalable bags for your camera and extra batteries.
- Make sure that you choose quality hiking boots and that you break them in before you hike to Machu Picchu.
- Pack blister patches, extra socks, and gel insoles.
- Wearing elastic knee braces may be helpful for those who are traveling this trail for the first time.
- Pack a small set of binoculars so you can see all of the ruins.
- Make sure that you pack snacks and a personal water bottle for the trip.
- Bring a walking stick with extra tips if your travel company says it is okay to bring along, but make sure you check with your travel company first because some of them do not allow walking sticks along the trail.
- Pack a headlamp with extra batteries so you are able to see in the dim forest.
- Pack a small first aid kit that includes band aids, anti-inflammatory medication, and any medications you take on a regular basis.
- Remember that the hike to Machu Picchu is a difficult hike but like a woman giving birth to a baby once you reach Machu Picchu and see the beauty it has to offer you will forget about how hard it was for you to get there.

- Always expect the unexpected from the weather when hiking to Machu Picchu. The day may start out warm and sunny but can quickly change to foggy, rainy, and cold.

- Pack toilet paper and hand sanitizer. There are no toilets available along the trail. What is available is a hut with a hole dug in the ground for you to do your business. They do not provide toilet paper! There is also no running water so you want to make sure you pack plenty of hand sanitizer to keep yourself healthy while on the hike

In the next chapter you will learn about all the things you can see and do once you reach Machu Picchu. Some of these will require you to buy tickets so if it is something that you think you would enjoy make sure you get your tickets before hand because only a limited number of people are allowed each day!

Chapter 5
Things to see and do in Machu Picchu

Even with all that was mentioned on the trails there is still more to see and do in Machu Picchu. In this section of the chapter we are going to discuss the attractions in Machu Picchu.

Wayna Picchu

Also spelled Huayna Picchu is located at the back of the Machu Picchu ruins. This is the most popular of the short walks available around Machu Picchu.

Huayna Picchu offers what many call "Dead Man's Stairs" which are literally stairs that are nothing more than rocks sticking out the side of a cliff. You must be very careful in wet weather because these stairs become dangerously slick.

Taking you through a short section the hike only lasts between 45 and 90 minutes. At first glance it may seem that the hike is difficult but it not really hard and the view is definitely worth the hike.

A Secret Temple

If you are one of the lucky 400 who get to travel to Huayna Picchu, make sure that you do not just climb up, take a few photos and climb back down. There is a secret temple you can hike to. The temple is called the temple of the moon and is on the far side of Huayna Picchu.

You will find a ceremonial shrine that was built into the cave along with many niches that are assumed to have held mummies at one time.

The Little Known Museum

There is an amazing museum at the base of Machu Picchu that very few ever visit or even know about. Museo de Sitio Manuel Chávez Ballón has an 8 dollar entry fee and fills in all the missing information about Machu Picchu.

From understanding why the Incas chose the spot they did to build Machu Picchu to filling in the blanks about why Macho Picchu was built, this amazing museum offers displays in both Spanish and English.

Museo de Sitio Manuel Chávez Ballón is about a 30 minute walk from Aguas Calientes and is located at the end of a long dirt road.

Intihuatana

Is the ritual stone found in Machu Picchu located at the top of the Intihuatana hill, and the name is from the Quechua language meaning to tie up the sun. On March 21 and September 21 at midday the sun lines up with the Intihuatana and there is no shadow cast. When this happens it looks as if the sun is standing on the pillar. Many people get confused and call this a sun dial and although the purpose for it is unclear, it is far more than just a giant sun dial. Many believe that it was used for religious purposes.

Central Plaza

At the back of Intihuatana there is a stair case that will decent to the central plaza. The central plaza is known as the green island amidst the stone structures. Many visitors report seeing llamas grazing or roaming through the grass.

Prison Group

At the lower end of the central plaza is an area called the prison group which consist of complex cell, niches, and passageways that are situated both above and below the ground.

Temple of the condor

At the center of the prison group is a temple which has been called the temple of the condor because of the amazing carving of a head of a condor with outstretched wings. The carving was created out of a natural rock formation that the Incas shaped into the wings of the condor. The head and neck of the condor are carved out of a rock on the floor of the temple. Historians believe that the head of the condor was used as a sacrificial alter. Under the temple is a cave that is believed to have held mummies.

Phuyupatamarka

When you come to the end of the Inca Trail you will be at a place called Phuyupatamarka which means the Town Above the Clouds. At 11,811ft above sea level this beautiful town can only be reached on foot and contains a chain of ceremonial baths. All of which have water running through them. There is also a ridge which offers a great camping site. If you camp on the ridge and rise at 3 am the next morning you will make it to Machu Picchu in time to see the sun rising through the sun gate.

Sacred Plaza

If you follow the stairs above the baths at Phuyupatamarka you will find a flat area with a bunch of rocks that was once used as a quarry. If you turn right at the top of the stairs passing the quarry you will find a short path which will lead to the Sacred Plaza. The Sacred Plaza is a four sided building that contains a small viewing platform on the curved wall. From this viewing platform you will be able to see the snowy peaks of Cordillera Vilcabamba and the roaring Río Urubamba below you.

Temple of the three windows

Important buildings border the Sacred Plaza on the remaining three sides and one of these buildings is called the Temple of the three windows. Given its name because of the three huge trapezoid shaped windows it contains, the temple has more elaborate carvings than those found in other houses. It is believed that there were originally five windows in the temple but two of them were closed up after the building of the temple.

Intipunku

Also called the sun gate is the end of the Inca Trail. The sun gate is made up of steps and many believe that it was used as a gate to control who entered the temple.

The Principle Temple

Situated in Machu Picchu, The Principle Temple got its name because of its massive size. On the western side of the temple is a kite shaped rock that is pointing south, this is said to represent the Southern Cross. There is also a much smaller temple that adjoins the Principle Temple which has been said was used for the priests to prepare for the religious ceremonies. There is damage to the right rear corner of the temple which was caused by the ground settling, not due to a fault in the architectural design.

Sacristy

Sacristy is the name of the smaller temple that is adjoining the Principle Temple. Inside the Sacristy you will find that there are many well carved niches in the walls that are believed to have held ceremonial objects. There is also a bench in the Sacristy that is carved out of stone. The Sacristy is most well-known for the two rocks bordering the entry. Each of these two rocks is said to contain 32 angles but when you try to count them all it is very easy to come up with different numbers each time.

Hut of the Caretaker of the Funerary Rock

The Inca trail enters Machu Picchu just below this hut which is one of the few buildings that has been restored with a thatched roof. Many researchers believe that the carved rock located behind the hut may have been used in mummifying the nobility of Machu Picchu. You must climb a zigzagged stair case in order to reach the Hut of the Caretaker of the Funerary Rock and if you continue on without climbing the stair case you will reach the 16 ceremonial baths.

Inca Drawbridge

Just a 20 minute hike from the caretakers hut you will be able to view the Inca Drawbridge. The area is mostly over run with vegetation but the hike is fairly level. You must be careful though because the trail is very narrow. The Inca Drawbridge is impassible today but the drawbridge shows the amazing architecture that the Incas were capable of.

Temple of the sun

The temple of the sun is by far one of the most recognized of the ruins in Machu Picchu. The temple of the sun is built on a solid granite rock and is in the shape of a semi-circle with a diameter of about 34 feet. The temple of the sun also contains two trapezoid shaped windows that have knobs protruding out of each corner. Just to the west of the temple of the sun is a rectangular shaped patio that contains nine ceremonial doors. The temple is located in the center of the eastern sector and was highly protected in the time of the Incas.

Royal Tomb

Below the temple of the sun, the royal tomb is almost hidden. The royal tomb is a cave that was carved out by Inca stonemasons and the purpose of the cave is highly debated but most anthropologists who have studies the stories surrounding the tomb believe that it was used for the highest offices of nobility although no mummies were ever found in it.

House of the high priest

Located directly across from the principle temple is the house of the high priest. Unlike the two temples in the sacred plaza, the house of the high priest has four walls and is a well-built solid structure. It is unclear if the priest lived here only during certain holy periods or if he was a full time resident. No one really knows what the tradition was.

Highlights of the Machu Picchu Region

In this section of the chapter I want to discuss the amazing attractions in the Machu Picchu region.

Baños Termales Cocalmayo

These spectacular hot springs truly are a world class attraction. The pools that washed out when the river flooded in 2010 have been rebuilt although the campground was not. You can catch a bus to the hot springs at around three pm when they go to collect the travelers from the Incan Trail, otherwise you will have to pay a taxi to get you there. As if amazing hot springs were not enough, you even have the opportunity to grab yourself a beer and a snack while visiting Baños Termales Cocalmayo.

Huancacalle

Is best known as the jumping off point for many treks to Vilcabamba but there are other treks available. The hikes can last anywhere from three to ten days with destinations such as Puncuyo, Inca Tambo, Choquequirau and Machu Picchu. The largest building in Huancacalle is the Hostal Manco Sixpac which is run by a local family of guides and is the only building in town that has hot water.

Just an hour's walk up the hill and you will be able to see the huge Manco Incas fortress Rosaspata. From there you can visit the sacred white rock of Yurac Rumi. The entire hike taken at a leisurely pace only takes three hours to complete.

Vilcabamba

This is the real lost city of the Incas that Bingham was searching for when he found Machu Picchu. The hike to Vilcabamba is long taking between three to nine days and rugged. The trek is a low altitude one though only reaching heights of 1000 feet above sea level it contains many steep accents as well as descents and you want to ensure you have a very experienced guide to take you on this trek.

Hotels:

There are many hotels available for you to stay in that are very close to Machu Picchu if you do not want to camp out. The prices range from $30USD per night to just over $500USD per night.

There is also one hotel that you can stay at for $900USD per night and it is the only hotel located adjacent to the Machu Picchu ruins.

Restaurants:

With over 100 restaurants available in Cusco you will not search long for a place to dine. One local favorite that is not found by many tourist is called the Tree House Restaurant. Known by those who find it as a hidden gem, it is located in Aguas Calientes up a steep hike. Known for its great atmosphere and fair prices along with amazing food, this is one gem that you do not want to miss out on when you are visiting Machu Picchu.

What you need to know

When you visit Machu Picchu you are not allowed to walk on the walls of any of the buildings. Doing so could cause the walls to collapse, loosen the stone work and ensure prompt whistle blowing from the guards on duty.

You should also be aware that it is against the law to stay the night at Machu Picchu and no one is allowed to enter after closing time. The guards to a thorough check each night to ensure no one tries to stay at Machu Picchu.

Limited Number of People

Recently the government put restrictions on the number of people who could enter Machu Picchu each day. On any given day Machu Picchu is only allowed to have 2500 visitors. Due to this restriction you are no longer allowed to buy tickets to enter Machu Picchu at the gate and must purchase them at the official ticket office in Cusco or online.

Chapter 6
Traveling to Machu Picchu

Now that you know everything there is to know about Machu Picchu, I want to discuss all of your options in Machu Picchu.

How to choose a Machu Picchu tour

Trying to select a tour company for a trip to Machu Picchu can seem overwhelming but you have to understand that not all of the tour companies are equal. If you want to ensure that you have the best time possible while you are in Peru, there are a few questions that you need to ask yourself.

1. Do you want to travel alone or are you okay with traveling in groups? Machu Picchu is a huge tourist attraction but if you are the kind of person who enjoys being alone it is possible in Machu Picchu. You also have the option of joining larger groups for trail hikes and such. If you are traveling on your own you will need to book your own flight to Cusco, purchase your entry tickets for Machu Picchu, as well as your train tickets to Aguas Calientes. Finally taking a bus the rest of the way to Machu Picchu. If you are the kind of person who does not like preplanning things, this may not be the best option for you.

2. Do you want to hike the Inca Trail to Machu Picchu? You should decide this very early on because the preparation for the trip is much more demanding if you chose to hike the trail. If you want to hike Inca Trail, you have to travel with a tour group and certified guide. Due to the fact that there are only 500 people allowed on this trail per day, you must have your permits approved in advance. As discussed earlier in this book, there are several other trails that you can take that follow ancient paths and are sprinkled with ruin sites. These trails are less crowed than the "traditional" Inca trail.

Choosing the company you will travel with.

The old saying "You get what you pay for" is still true to this day but it pays to shop around when traveling to Machu Picchu because there are hundreds of companies that give tours and you want to ensure that you get the best deal.

You also want to ensure that your experience is worth the expense. If you book with small local operators you will definitely save money but the quality of the tour is not always guaranteed. This is a great option for those who travel to Cusco without making any prior plans but it is recommended if you do not speak Spanish to speak to your guide ahead of time to ensure there will be no communication barriers. You should also be sure that you check to see what equipment is provided for your trip as well because some of the smaller companies do not provide the same equipment as the larger ones. And as discussed in previous chapters, you don't want to get on the Inca trail and realize you have no food or sleeping bag.

Larger companies with of course cost you more but your money will also be more secure. International companies usually offer travel insurance, online payment options, and all inclusive trips. All inclusive trips cover air fare, transfers, and support services. These companies usually work with the smaller local companies that have been assessed for quality.

A great way to ensure that you chose a good company who provides English speaking agents is to simply call the company and start asking them questions regarding the trip.

Variables you must prepare for when traveling to Machu Picchu

1. Altitude. Machu Picchu is located 7970 feet above sea level, and altitude sickness can affect everyone young or old. The symptoms of altitude sickness are: Headache, Loss of appetite, Nausea, Upset stomach, and Difficulty sleeping. One way to acclimate yourself to the altitude is to spend a few days in Cusco which is located 11200 above sea level. Then after a few days in Cusco you can press on to Machu Picchu but make sure that you do not drink too much alcohol or take part in a lot of strenuous activity. If the altitude sickness gets too bad, you can ask your hotel for extra oxygen or seek medical care immediately.

2. The Sun! Don't let the lush greenery surrounding Machu Picchu fool you, when you are at such high altitudes, it is very easy for you to get sun brunt. And you may not even feel the power of the sun until it is too late. Make sure you wear sunscreen while you are in Machu Picchu along with long sleeves and long pants. This will ensure that you are not burnt by the sun.

3. Mosquitos. Going to Machu Picchu is a trip that you should be able to remember for the rest of your life. You should not have to look back and remember being attacked by hundreds of blood sucking bugs. Due to the moisture in the air, mosquitos are thick in Machu Picchu and usually come out mid-afternoon to feast on the visitors. You should make sure their meals do not include you by applying some mosquito or bug spray before you enter Machu Picchu. The long pants and long sleeves you wear to avoid sunburn will help with mosquitos also.

4. Price gouging. Prices in Machu Picchu are always higher during the tour season but there are some people who will go as far as doubling their prices in order to take advantage of unsuspecting tourists. The way to

avoid this is to shop around if you are going to buy anything in Machu Picchu to ensure that you are getting the best price possible.

Make sure you carry your passport with you.

Along with your entrance ticket to Machu Picchu, you will need to bring your passport. You will not be allowed to enter Machu Picchu without a passport. When you leave Machu Picchu to have a snack, drink, or use the bathroom you will have to show your passport to regain entry into Machu Picchu. There is an unmarked stand just outside of the gates to Machu Picchu where you can have your passport stamped with the Machu Picchu stamp.

What will you do with your luggage?

No luggage is allowed in Machu Picchu. Most hotels will offer a free service to hold your luggage for you while you visit Machu Picchu but if you are not staying in a hotel you will have to leave your luggage at the luggage storage area just outside of the gates. You will also have to pay a fee for leaving your luggage here.

You are also not allowed to eat or drink inside the ruins. Although it is against the rules to carry any food or drink inside of the ruins most do not have a problem as long as they leave the ruins before they eat or drink anything. There is nowhere in Machu Picchu that will allow you to buy snacks or drinks so it is imperative if you are planning on spending the day there that you pack snacks and water.

You are ready to go to Machu Picchu

You now know everything that you need to know in order to have an amazing trip and rediscover Machu Picchu for yourself. If you are planning on traveling to Machu Picchu, it would be a great idea for you to take this book with you so that you have a great reference guide and do not miss out on anything that Machu Picchu or the surrounding areas have to offer. I hope you have enjoyed reading this book as much as I have enjoyed writing it and I hope that you have amazing journeys ahead of you in Machu Picchu.

Conclusion

Thank you again for downloading this book!

Finally, if you enjoyed this book, please take the time to share your thoughts and post a review on Amazon. It'd be greatly appreciated!

Thank you and good luck!

Check Out My Other Books

Below you'll find some of my other popular books that are popular on Amazon and Kindle as well. Simply click on the links below to check them out. Alternatively, you can visit my author page on Amazon to see other work done by me.

If the links do not work, for whatever reason, you can simply search for these titles on the Amazon website to find them.

Printed in Great Britain
by Amazon.co.uk, Ltd.,
Marston Gate.